REGIONS OF THE UNITED STATES

EXPLORE THE WEST

by Kristine Spanier, MLIS

pogo

Ideas for Parents and Teachers

Pogo Books let children practice reading informational text while introducing them to nonfiction features such as headings, labels, sidebars, maps, and diagrams, as well as a table of contents, glossary, and index.

Carefully leveled text with a strong photo match offers early fluent readers the support they need to succeed.

Before Reading

- "Walk" through the book and point out the various nonfiction features. Ask the student what purpose each feature serves.
- Look at the glossary together. Read and discuss the words.

Read the Book

- Have the child read the book independently.
- Invite him or her to list questions that arise from reading.

After Reading

- Discuss the child's questions. Talk about how he or she might find answers to those questions.
- Prompt the child to think more. Ask: Have you been to any states in the West? Which states would you like to see?

Pogo Books are published by Jump!
5357 Penn Avenue South
Minneapolis, MN 55419
www.jumplibrary.com

Library of Congress Cataloging-in-Publication Data

Names: Spanier, Kristine, author.
Title: Explore the West / Kristine Spanier.
Description: Minneapolis: Jump!, Inc., 2023.
Series: Regions of the United States
Includes index. | Audience: Ages 7-10
Identifiers: LCCN 2021058480 (print)
LCCN 2021058481 (ebook)
ISBN 9781636907291 (hardcover)
ISBN 9781636907307 (paperback)
ISBN 9781636907314 (ebook)
Subjects: LCSH: West (U.S.)–Juvenile literature.
Classification: LCC F591 .S727 2023 (print)
LCC F591 (ebook) | DDC 978–dc23/eng/20211214
LC record available at https://lccn.loc.gov/2021058480
LC ebook record available at https://lccn.loc.gov/2021058481

Editor: Jenna Gleisner
Designer: Molly Ballanger

Photo Credits: Bertl123/Shutterstock, cover (left); Chones/Shutterstock, cover (right); Felix Mizioznikov/Shutterstock, cover (bottom); acavemancandoit/Shutterstock, 1; Jillian Cooper/iStock, 3; GraphicaArtis/Getty, 4; Bettmann/Getty, 5; North Wind Picture Archives/Alamy, 6-7; Universal Images Group/SuperStock, 8-9; Andriy Blokhin/Shutterstock, 10; Rachel Doreen/Shutterstock, 11; ALong/Shutterstock, 12-13tl; Lynn Yeh/Shutterstock, 12-13tr; EKPhotos307/Shutterstock, 12-13bl; melissamn/Shutterstock, 12-13br; Jim Cumming/Shutterstock, 14-15tl; Gerald Corsi/iStock, 14-15tr; Milan Zygmunt/Shutterstock, 14-15bl; Tory Kallman/Shutterstock, 14-15br; Agnieszka Gaul/Shutterstock, 16; Eloi_Omella/iStock, 17; SvetlanaSF/Shutterstock, 18-19; saraporn/Shutterstock, 20-21t; LanaG/Shutterstock, 20-21b; Josemaria Toscano/Shutterstock, 22t; lucky-photographer/iStock, 22bl; Gary C. Tognoni/Shutterstock, 22br; canadastock/Shutterstock, 23.

Printed in the United States of America at Corporate Graphics in North Mankato, Minnesota.

Title Page Image: Glacier National Park, Montana

TABLE OF CONTENTS

CHAPTER 1

HISTORY AND LOCATION

For thousands of years before Europeans arrived, Indigenous people lived across North America. In the 1700s, Spain and France controlled land west of the Mississippi River. The United States bought this land in 1803. This was the Louisiana Purchase.

Meriwether Lewis and William Clark explored the West **Region**. From 1804 to 1806, they mapped a path to the Pacific Ocean. It was called the Oregon Trail. **Settlers** followed. They wanted land to farm. Some split off toward California.

In 1848, gold was discovered in California. Word got out. Gold is **valuable**. Others wanted to find it, too. Soon, around 300,000 more people arrived. This was called the Gold Rush.

TAKE A LOOK!

California is part of the West. What other states are part of this region? Take a look!

Alaska
Hawaii

The West is the biggest region in the country. Some states border Canada. California borders Mexico.

Alaska and Hawaii are the only states that are not part of the **contiguous** United States. Alaska is the biggest state in the West. It is also the biggest in the country. Hawaii is a group of islands. It is in the Pacific Ocean.

WHAT DO YOU THINK?

Alaska became a state in 1959. So did Hawaii. They were the last states added to the country. Do you know when your state became a state? If not, how can you find out?

CHAPTER 2

GEOGRAPHY AND WILDLIFE

The West is filled with many **landforms**. The Rocky Mountains are here. They stretch more than 3,000 miles (4,800 kilometers) from Canada to New Mexico.

Rocky Mountains

Great Salt Lake is in Utah. Three rivers carry salt to it. The lake has more than 4 billion tons of salt in it! This makes it easy to float in the water.

Yellowstone National Park is the oldest U.S. national park. It is in Wyoming, Montana, and Idaho. A **volcano** is under the park. It heats the water features in the park.

DID YOU KNOW?

Active volcanoes are in many states in the West. Hawaii's Mauna Loa is the biggest. Mount St. Helens is in Washington. It **erupted** on May 18, 1980. Lives were lost. More than 10 million trees were destroyed.

geyser

hot spring

mud pot

steam vent

cougar

grizzly bear

Gila monster

orca

Cougars prowl the mountains in the West. Grizzly bears catch salmon in Alaska. Gila monsters hunt in the Mojave Desert. Orcas swim off the Pacific Coast.

CHAPTER 3

DAILY LIFE

The Space Needle is in Seattle, Washington. It is 605 feet (184 meters) tall. You can ride up in an elevator. The top spins. From it, you can see the city. You can see Mount Rainier, too. It is the tallest mountain in the contiguous United States.

Los Angeles, California, is the second most **populated** U.S. city. Many movies are made in Hollywood.

Farmers in the West raise **livestock**. They grow fruits and vegetables. Many people work in **tourism**. Why? Travelers visit to see the sights.

San Francisco, California

TAKE A LOOK!

What are some of the West's top **industries**? Take a look!

= business
= entertainment
= farming
= fishing
= manufacturing
= maritime transport
= mining
= oil and gas production
= technology
= tourism
= wood products

Much of the West is warm. Death Valley is a desert in California. It is the driest and hottest place in North America. The region's mountains are much cooler. They get snow in winter!

The West is **vast**. Would you like to explore it?

WHAT DO YOU THINK?

Hawaii is **tropical**. Parts of it get more than 450 inches (11,430 millimeters) of rain a year. Alaska is the coldest state. Some areas get 40 feet (12 m) of snow each year. Would you like to live in either of these states? Why or why not?

Death Valley

Colorado

QUICK FACTS

WEST REGION

Location: western United States

Population (2021 estimate): 69,274,941

Most Populated City in Each State:
Anchorage, AK
Los Angeles, CA
Denver, CO
Honolulu, HI
Boise, ID
Billings, MT
Las Vegas, NV
Portland, OR
Salt Lake City, UT
Seattle, WA
Cheyenne, WY

PORTLAND, OR

MONUMENT VALLEY, UT

DEVIL'S TOWER, WY

Top Industries: entertainment, farming, fishing, forestry, maritime transportation, mining, tourism

Average High Temperature (contiguous United States): 59 degrees Fahrenheit (15 degrees Celsius) (California)

Average Low Temperature (contiguous United States): 42 degrees Fahrenheit (6 degrees Celsius) (Wyoming)

Major Landforms: Cascade Mountains, Death Valley, Rocky Mountains, Mojave Desert, Sierra Nevada Mountains, Teton Mountains, Mauna Loa, Mount St. Helens, Mount Rainier

Highest Point: Mount Denali, AK, 20,310 feet (6,190 m)

Major Waterways: Arctic Ocean, Bering Sea, Gulf of Alaska, Missouri River, Yukon River, Rio Grande River, Colorado River, Great Salt Lake, Lake Tahoe, Pacific Ocean

Major Landmarks: Devil's Tower, Glacier National Park, Golden Gate Bridge, Hoover Dam, Monument Valley, Space Needle, Yellowstone National Park

GLOSSARY

contiguous: Touching without another country or body of water coming between.

erupted: Suddenly and violently threw out lava, hot ash, and steam.

Indigenous: Of or relating to the earliest known people to live in a place.

industries: Businesses or trades.

landforms: Natural features of land surfaces.

livestock: Animals that are kept or raised on a farm or ranch.

populated: Having people living in it.

region: A general area or a specific district or territory.

settlers: People who make a home or live in a new place.

tourism: The business of serving people who are traveling for pleasure.

tropical: Of or having to do with the hot, rainy area of the tropics.

valuable: Worth a lot of money.

vast: Very large.

volcano: A mountain with openings through which molten lava, ash, and hot gases can erupt.

Hoover Dam, Nevada

INDEX

TO LEARN MORE

Finding more information is as easy as 1, 2, 3.

1. Go to www.factsurfer.com
2. Enter "exploretheWest" into the search box.
3. Choose your book to see a list of websites.

FACT SURFER